Cryptocurrency

*How to Make Money with Bitcoin -
The Investor's Guide to Bitcoin Mining,
Trading, Blockchain, and Smart
Contracts*

by

David Blake

Table of Contents

validity or interim quality. Trademarks that are mentioned are done without written consent and can in no way be considered an endorsement from the trademark holder.

The author of this book has taken careful measures to share vital information about the subject. May its readers acquire the right knowledge, wisdom, inspiration, and succeed.

Introduction

These days, bitcoin is continuously gaining popularity and public acceptance. Many people want to learn how Bitcoin works and hope to find their way to financial freedom. In fact, the majority of those who use bitcoin do not actually use it as a substitute for money. Instead, they see bitcoin as a lucrative investment, and for good reason. The value of bitcoin has been constantly increasing over the years. As of November 2017, the price of 1 bitcoin has reached more than USD 8,000, and it is only climbing higher. Although bitcoin is also subject to the usual fluctuations in price, if you look at its long-term price movement, it is easy to recognize that it is a very profitable investment.

Before any person can take advantage of what bitcoin offers, you need to have a good foundation and understanding of what bitcoin is really all about. The following chapters will teach you the ins and outs of bitcoin. You will learn more about Bitcoin and its brief history. You will also get knowledge about what cryptocurrency and blockchain technology are that you are going to be able to use for a wide variety of lucrative purposes in the near future.

Bitcoin is continuously improving. We will tackle what the pros and cons of using Bitcoin are to ensure you get started on the right foot. Knowing about these will help you avoid the common mistakes that many new investors make, and prosper where they have burnt out early. As you continue reading this book, you will be guided on how you can effectively make money through Bitcoin. Soon, you will understand why thousands of new investors put their trust in Bitcoin every single day.

Bitcoin's development has been really fascinating, in less than a decade it has grown from an online novelty into a world-changing economic powerhouse. No wonder why many people all around the globe are now trusting this new digital currency. To see where things might be going in the future, we will also discuss Bitcoin's likely future as well.

Chapter 1:

Bitcoin Basics

What is Bitcoin?

Bitcoin is a digital currency that is held and stored electronically. It functions as a substitute for money. It also has a decentralized network. This means that no central authority or government controls it. Remember, Bitcoin does not have a physical existence; it only exists online.

Bitcoin is the most popular and successful cryptocurrency in the world. As of November 22, 2017, the price of 1 Bitcoin is around $8,179 (USD).

Bitcoin is accepted and used by different merchants worldwide: The gaming platform, Steam, accepts bitcoins. The giant computer software, Microsoft, also accepts payment in bitcoins. The company engaged in space tourism

Cryptocurrency

known as Virgin Galactic also accepts bitcoins. Overstock and even some sellers on Shopify accept payments in bitcoins. Many individuals and merchants use Bitcoin. The good news is that with the increasing popularity of the Bitcoin cryptocurrency, more and more people and businesses are being open to the idea of using Bitcoin.

Cryptocurrency

The term *cryptocurrency* refers to a digital asset that is secured by cryptography. Cryptography is the process of securing information. The application of cryptography can be traced back to the time of the Second World War when it was important to ensure that information and communication between and among the parties are secured and would not be disclosed to the enemy. After some time, cryptography found its application in cryptocurrency by converting information into codes that are almost uncrackable, which can then be used to track purchases and all other transactions. To date, there are more than 900 cryptocurrencies that have already been created. Creating a new cryptocurrency is easy. In fact, a basic knowledge in C++ will allow you to generate your own cryptocurrency in just a few days. The problem is that it is not easy to effectively promote a cryptocurrency, much less to convince people to take interest and use or invest in your cryptocurrency.

You can consider cryptocurrency as the primary Internet money since it is stored and transacted online. Keep in mind that cryptocurrencies like Bitcoin are not considered legal tender. Therefore, they are not a medium of payment that can be used by a debtor to compel his creditor to accept payment, except if payment in cryptocurrency is stated in the contract. The good news is that although cryptocurrencies are not considered as legal tender, many individuals and businesses are still open to the use of cryptocurrencies like Bitcoin.

Brief history of Bitcoin

In August of 2008, the domain name, *bitcoin.org*, was registered. After a few months, a paper entitled *Bitcoin: A Peer-to-Peer Electronic Cash System* was published on a cryptography mailing list under the pseudonym, Satoshi Nakamoto. In January 2009, Bitcoin was finally introduced in the market.

Cryptocurrency

It was also Satoshi Nakamoto who mined the first block of the Bitcoin chain, known as the *genesis block*, and for which he received 50 bitcoins. One of the early supporters of Bitcoin was a man named Hal Finney. On the same day when Bitcoin was released, Mr. Finney downloaded the bitcoin software, and for which he received 10 bitcoins from Satoshi Nakamoto. Said transaction is considered the very first bitcoin transaction in history. Even to this day, the true identity of Satoshi Nakamoto remains a mystery.

It is estimated that Satoshi Nakamoto had mined millions worth of bitcoins before he disappeared from the public. Some say that Satoshi Nakamoto was Hal Finney himself, while others claim that Nakamoto was composed of a group of computer experts. There have been many views and theories on the true identity of Satoshi Nakamoto yet no one can absolutely guarantee the real person or people behind one of the world's revolutionizing technologies, Bitcoin.

Another interesting bitcoin transaction in history was the purchase of two pizzas for 10,000 bitcoins. Back then, Bitcoin did not have a huge value. However, Bitcoin has grown significantly over time. A classic example to illustrate this point is this: If only you had invested even just $500 in bitcoins back in 2009 or 2010, then you would have been a multimillionaire by now. The good news is that even today, the price of bitcoin is continuously increasing.

Blockchain

The blockchain, originally referred to as *block chain*(two words), is the backbone technology of Bitcoin. The block is a form of a public, decentralized, and distributed ledger. It also has high security. Every block or record on the chain is connected to a previous block. This means that any change or modification made to any block will affect the whole blockchain system. This connection between and among the different blocks on the chain ensures that all records are legitimate, honest, and secure.

In a blockchain, the records are distributed and spread across a vast network of computers. To successfully attack a blockchain, a hacker will need to have at least 51% of the total hash rate or computing power of the entire network. This is the concept of the 51% attack. Since Bitcoin has a very broad network, it also has a very high hash rate, which makes it virtually unhackable.

The Bitcoin blockchain is a public blockchain, which means that all bitcoin transactions are verifiable and viewable to everyone. This is to ensure fairness and integrity of the records.

Be aware that in bitcoin's blockchain system, confirmed transactions could no longer be canceled, altered, modified, or withdrawn. Hence, be very careful with every input that you make.

The blockchain technology is not only applicable to bitcoin. Many experts have discovered that the blockchain technology can actually be used for other financial services, and even for non-financial purposes.

Is there a private blockchain?

When people talk about the blockchain technology, they always perceive it as something that is public because this is how bitcoin's blockchain is structured. What many people are not aware of is that there is also another kind of blockchain known as a private blockchain. Unlike a public blockchain, a private blockchain has a central authority or organization that has control and power over the entire blockchain system. This specialized authority or group can change, add, and remove, transactions over the blockchain network even without the consent of everyone in the network. As you can see, this is something that can be abused. This kind of blockchain is good for the use of private companies or between and among known and trusted parties. This kind of blockchain is not recommended for any cryptocurrency as it can be used to unduly influence the records. Fortunately, bitcoin's blockchain system is a public blockchain, so you can rest assured that all the records are fair, safe, and genuine.

Bitcoin transaction process

How does a bitcoin transaction work? There are three main elements of a transaction, namely: The input, recipient's wallet address, and the amount. Let us take a closer look at them one by one:

➢ Input

Before you can start sending bitcoins to anyone, you must first have bitcoins in your bitcoin wallet. Thisis referred to as the input.

It is the bitcoins in the bitcoin wallet of the sender. For example, if A will send 10 bitcoins to B, then A needs to have at least 10 bitcoins in his bitcoin wallet.

➢ Recipient's wallet address

This refers to the wallet address where you will send bitcoins. You should know your recipient's bitcoin wallet address. A wallet address is like a string of random letters and numbers.

➢ Amount

This simply refers to the amount that is involved in the transaction. In our example, the amount involved is 10 bitcoins. Make sure that you input the correct amount as it is impossible to cancel a transaction once it has been confirmed.

Smart contracts

Smart contracts are computer protocols that function to ensure, verify, and facilitate the negotiation and performance of contracts between the parties. Once certain conditions are met, then smart contracts will handle the execution of a contract. Although smart contracts are only known to execute simple tasks only, you can use numerous smart contracts to handle more complicated tasks.

Bitcoin is not known for its ability to use and handle smart contracts. Among the many cryptocurrencies out there, Ethereum is the one that is known for making use of smart contracts. The Bitcoin protocol has already evolved and now supports the use of smart contracts. Although the functionality of bitcoin's smart contracts is not as programmable as it is on Ethereum, certain functionality can still be made using bitcoin scripting.

Smart contracts are self-executing contracts. As long as the terms and conditions are met, then you can rest assured that the contract will be executed to the letter. Smart contracts allow transactions to take place even between anonymous parties.

The idea of a smart contract can be traced back in 1994. A proposal was made by a computer scientist named, Nick Szabo. He was also the inventor of Bit Gold, a type of virtual currency which was introduced in 1998. Yes, bitcoin was not the first cryptocurrency that was introduced in the market. According to Szabo, "These new securities are formed by combining securities (such as bonds) and derivatives (options and futures) in a wide variety of ways. Very complex term structures for payments can now be built into standardized contracts and traded with low transaction costs, due to computerized analysis of these complex term structures."

Other cryptocurrencies

There are more than 900 different cryptocurrencies that have already been created, and new cryptocurrencies are continuously being introduced in the market. Although there are many different kinds of cryptocurrencies out there, only a few can attract the market's attention and interest. Bitcoin remains to be the number one cryptocurrency in the world. In fact, it is the leading standard that all other cryptocurrencies have been categorized as *altcoins*, which is short for alternative coins. Let us take a look at some of the notable altcoins in the world:

➢ Ethereum

Ethereum was launched in 2015. It is currently the second most successful cryptocurrency in the world next to bitcoin. Some people even claim that Ethereum will soon overtake Bitcoin, although this seems far from happening. Ethereum uses smart contracts and Distributed Applications. Ethereum applications run using Ethereum's own platform cryptographic token known as *ether*. As of November 22, 2017, the price of 1 ether is around USD 365.

➢ Litecoin

Litecoin is not a new player in the cryptocurrency market. It was launched in 2011 and became one of the early competitors of bitcoin. Litecoin functions just like bitcoin, and it aims to be the "better" version of bitcoin. It claims to have a higher block generation rate, which means that it can confirm transactions much faster than bitcoin. There is also a growing number of businesses that accept Litecoin. As of November 22, 2017, the price of 1 Litecoin is around USD 70.

Cryptocurrency

➢ Ripple

Unlike other cryptocurrencies that seem to take the place of banks, Ripple actually works mutually with banks. It "enables banks to settle cross-border payments in real time, with end-to-end transparency, and at lower costs." It was launched in 2012 and is slowly gaining market capitalization. As of November 22, 2017, the price of 1 Ripple is around USD 0.23.

➢ Zcash

Zcash was launched in the latter part of 2016. This is how Zcash defines itself: "If Bitcoin is like http for money, Zcash is https," and the reason is that Zcash offers more privacy than Bitcoin. When you use Zcash, you will be offered a choice to use *shielded transactions.* Using advanced cryptography, shielded transactions will make private the details as to the sender, recipient, and even the amount involved in a transaction. As of November 22, 2017, the price of 1 Zcash is around USD 290.

➤ Monero

Monero was launched in 2014. It has drawn lots of interest in the cryptocurrency community. In fact, it is the only cryptocurrency that is purely donation-based. Its main focus is on decentralization and scalability. It also allows its users to enjoy improved privacy by using its unique feature known as *ring signatures*. When you use ring signatures, a legitimate transaction that you make is mixed up with fake or invalid transactions. Hence, when people look at the public blockchain, it will be hard to tell which transaction is valid and those that are not real. This way the real transaction (your transaction) will be "hidden." As of November 22, 2017, the price of 1 Monero is around USD 146.

There are many other cryptocurrencies in the world. The list above is only to give you an idea of other famous cryptocurrencies. As you can see, to compete with bitcoin, altcoins have additional features to make them appear more valuable. Gone are the days when you can just introduce a cryptocurrency in the market and expect a good following. To attract attention and interest, you need to focus on effective promotion and give value to the market. Still, it is worth stressing the fact that among all the cryptocurrencies in the world, Bitcoin remains the be the number one and most successful cryptocurrency, with a price of around USD 8,179 as of November 22, 2017 — and its price is continuously increasing.

Legality of using bitcoin

Although Bitcoin is unregulated and decentralized, it does not mean that the state cannot impose regulations or restrictions on its use. After all, a state has the primary responsibility of protecting its people and promoting the general welfare. Generally, the use of bitcoins is legal but there are a few states like Ecuador and Bolivia where the use of bitcoin and other cryptocurrencies is outlawed.

It is not hard to understand why the use of bitcoin and other cryptocurrencies is considered illegal in some states. Due to the level of anonymity enjoyed by cryptocurrency users, it can be used in the commission of crimes like money laundering. Although most states do not totally outlaw the use of Bitcoin, certain security measures may be imposed, such as the Know Your Customer (KYC) policy, and others. Still, there are states like Singapore that do not impose any form of regulation on the use of Bitcoins or any other cryptocurrency. Before you start using bitcoins, it is suggested that you check the laws and rules of your state on the matter. The good news is that more and more states are being open to the idea of using cryptocurrency. In fact, Russia which previously outlawed the use of bitcoins is now one of the supporters of bitcoin. As time goes by, more and more people are being open and accept the use of Bitcoin.

How to earn bitcoins

Before you can make money with bitcoins, you should first have your own bitcoins. So, how do you earn bitcoins? The best way to earn your first bitcoins for investing is by buying bitcoins. There are hot wallets like Coinbase and coins.ph that will allow you to purchase bitcoins instantly using your Visa or Master card. You can also buy bitcoins from local and online bitcoin exchanges. You should be very careful when buying bitcoins. Do not forget that the price of bitcoin fluctuates significantly in a short period of time. Before you make any buy order, be sure to check the current price of bitcoin. Another good place to buy bitcoins is from cryptocurrency trading platforms. This means that you will have to sign up for a free account with a bitcoin trading broker. Do not worry; the signing up process can be completed in as fast as two minutes.

There are other ways to earn bitcoins, such as by mining, gambling, and others. All these are discussed in more detail later in the book. Another way to earn bitcoin is to request it as a mode of payment. After all, bitcoin is a substitute for money. This is easy to do, especially if you have an e-commerce or online business. Just give your bitcoin address to the customers, and you will be able to receive payments at any time. Still, when it comes to investing in bitcoins, the best and easiest way is simply to buy bitcoins just as anyone who wants to invest in stocks would have to buy stocks. It is worth repeating that before you buy bitcoins, you should first know the current price of bitcoin to be sure that you are getting a fair deal. There are many sites online that sell bitcoins at a very high price.

There are people who want to buy bitcoins using PayPal. The way to do this is by using another service known as Virwox. You should know that this is not a good way to buy bitcoins because the process is very expensive. Therefore, although this may seem convenient to you, this is not a suggested method.

Is it for you?

There are many ways to make money, and making money with bitcoin is probably not for everyone. Again, even though bitcoin continues to prove itself as a profitable investment, it is still an investment. This means that it is still vulnerable to certain risks, including the risk of losing all your money. If you are not the type who is willing to take risks, then bitcoin might not be for you. If you are willing to exert some hard work in research and are ready to face some risks, then investing in bitcoin might just be the best investment that you can make, for it is something that can completely change your life for the better.

Chapter 2:

Pros and Cons of Using Bitcoin

Pros

➢ Cannot be manipulated

Bitcoin has a decentralized network. It is not under the control of any central authority or government. Hence, it is not subject to any form of undue influence or manipulation. In fact, even the founder of Bitcoin, Satoshi Nakamoto, cannot alter or remove the records on bitcoin's blockchain. You can rest assured that the record of transactions is fair and free from any form of manipulation.

➢ Lower cost

The bitcoin blockchainis designed in a way that it effectively removes the middleman. You do not have to worry about banking fees or any other third-party fee. You can send and receive bitcoins over the bitcoin network without having to rely on any other service provider. This effectively cuts down your cost, especially if you intend to send or receive bitcoins on a regular basis.

➢ Anonymity

Bitcoin users enjoy a high level of anonymity. When you make a transaction, whether sending or receiving bitcoin, your name and other personal details will not be revealed. The only record that will appear on the blockchain would be your bitcoin wallet address, the bitcoin wallet address of the recipient, the amount involved, and a time stamp. All personal information will be kept private and confidential.

➢ Quick transactions

Unlike transacting with banks where you may have to wait for days for a check or transaction to clear, bitcoin transactions only takes a few minutes to complete. If you are willing to pay a small mining fee, then the transaction can be completed almost instantly. Such quick transaction feature is one of the main highlights of using bitcoins.

➢ Round the clock availability

The bitcoin network does not close. It is open and available 24/7, even during holidays. Feel free to send and receive bitcoin at any time you want. Unlike transacting with banks that are only available every weekday, the bitcoin network is always available.

➢ Profitable

Investing in bitcoin can be highly profitable. Let me remind you of a classic example: Had you invested even just $500 in bitcoin way back in 2009 or 2010, then you would have been a multimillionaire by now. Had you invested in bitcoin early in 2017, then you would have profited by more than 100% of your total investment by now. The gold need is that despite the already high value of bitcoin, it remains to be a lucrative investment. According to some experts, the value of bitcoin can be expected to increase by more than 300% within the next two years.

Cryptocurrency

➤ Convenient

Using bitcoins is very convenient. Everything happens online with just a few clicks of a mouse. You do not have to drive and visit your bank; all that you need to focus access the Internet using your computer or a mobile device, and you can make transactions easily and quickly.

Cons

➤ High volatility

The price of bitcoin fluctuates rapidly and significantly. It is not uncommon for its price to experience an increase or decrease of 10% in just 24 hours. This is one of the reasons why there are investors who are cautious of investing in bitcoin but it is also the high volatility of bitcoin that makes it an attractive investment. Due to its high volatiry, high price surges become possible.

➤ Technology risk

Although bitcoin is considered a good technology, there is a risk that a more competitive cryptocurrency may soon hit the market in such a way that bitcoin will lose its position as the number of cryptocurrency in the world.

It should also be noted that bitcoin's network runs on a very high hash rate considering the multitude of computer networks connected to it. There is a risk that the technology behind bitcoin may not be able to handle too much hash rate in the long run. Although bitcoin appears to be very advanced, it is still a fact that bitcoin, as well as the blockchain technology, is a fairly new kind of technology.

➢ Security risk

Although the blockchain prides itself on a high level of security, it does not mean that it is absolutely invulnerable to all forms of attack. There are also some experts who claim that the 51‰ attack concept is not absolute. In fact, since the bitcoin network is connected with one another, a successful attack on a single node or block can adversely affect the entire bitcoin blockchain. There are also some bitcoin wallets that have been hacked and compromised. When you use bitcoins, you should be aware of the best practices on how you can keep your bitcoin wallet safe and secure.

➢ Legal risk

At present, only a few states consider the use of bitcoin and other cryptocurrencies to be illegal, and only a few impose stringent regulations. This does not mean that governments will no longer regulate its use in the future. According to experts, governments may soon take stricter measures if more people switch to bitcoin and begin to stop using legal tender money (the money issued by the government). This is because such instance can cause a significant drop in the price of a state's official currency. This is a simple application of the law on supply and demand. If people turn to bitcoin and the demand for the state's official currency decreases, then you can expect for its price to drop, which will not be good for the economy. Also, due to the enhanced privacy and security enjoyed by bitcoin users, the state can take preventive and protective measures, especially if it has good reasons to believe that bitcoin is also being used for the commission of illegal activities.

Chapter 2: Pros and Cons of Using Bitcoin

➢ Market risk

Whether investing in stocks, realty, or cryptocurrency, one of the crucial factors to look for is the market. It is not just the price of bitcoin that is highly volatile, even the market behavior is also hard to predict. If the market suddenly changes its mind or preference and switches to another cryptocurrency or stops using cryptocurrency, then this can hurt the price of bitcoin.

Another common market risk is when investors are in a state of panic. For example, when China declared to close down all its local cryptocurrency exchanges, there was panic in the market, and investors cashed out their positions by making sell orders thinking that the price of bitcoin would take a massive drop. This resulted in a more significant decrease in the price of bitcoin that it was supposed to be. As you can see, how the market reacts to changes can have a serious effect on the price of bitcoin.

Cryptocurrency

> Competition

There is a tight level of competition among the different cryptocurrencies in the market. Not to mention, new cryptocurrencies are also being introduced in the market, and these cryptocurrencies also offer value and additional features. Although competition may be considered healthy as it compels businesses to improve and maintain a decent quality, it can also cause businesses or cryptocurrencies to lose their share in the market. To remain a profitable investment, bitcoin needs to maintain its edge and stay ahead of the competition.

The competition per se is not bad. In fact, it is an essential element in business to ensure the best quality of service. In the world of cryptocurrency, competition can be a problem as it can easily cause a certain cryptocurrency to lose market capitalization. It is quite surprising that although bitcoin does not offer additional value or features, it remains the number one cryptocurrency in the world.

Chapter 2: Pros and Cons of Using Bitcoin

Is it worth it?

When making any investment, you need to weigh the pros and cons and see if it is worth taking. This book teaches bitcoin but does not promote it in any way. Now, by simply looking at and comparing the pros and cons of bitcoin, as well as analyzing the things that are taking place in the market, it is not difficult to tell that bitcoin is worth taking as an investment. It has a high-profit potential. In fact, its profit potential is way higher than the usual investment opportunities like stocks, bonds, and realty. The good news is that the probability of making a profit is high. This is another thing that makes investing in bitcoin attractive. Unlike the regular kind of investment, if the profit potential is high, you can expect that the risk is also high. This is not how it works with bitcoin. When you invest in bitcoin, you know that you take ownership of something that many people consider as valuable. Another benefit is that most people believe that the value of bitcoin will continue to increase.

If you are still hesitant whether you should put your money in bitcoin or not, you can just test it for some time. Simply invest a small amount and see what happens. The important thing is to take action and grab the opportunity while it is still there. The truth is that some people in the world are earning lots of profit simply by investing their money in bitcoin. While bitcoin is still considered a hot topic and continuously draws attention, it is the best time to take advantage of it and rake in serious money.

Chapter 3:

Bitcoin Wallets

Before you can start to use bitcoins, you need a place where you can store them. You need to have a bitcoin wallet. There are many types of bitcoin wallets, and you need to understand their differences so that you will know which bitcoin wallet will best suit your needs.

Different types of Bitcoin wallets

Basically, there are two main categories of a bitcoin wallet: a hot wallet and a cold wallet. A hot wallet refers to the kind of bitcoin wallet that exists online or on the web, while a cold wallet is a kind of bitcoin wallet that exists offline. On the one hand, since a hot wallet exists online, it is more convenient to use than a cold wallet. On the other hand, a cold wallet offers more security than a hot wallet since it is not exposed to the Internet.

Cryptocurrency

Cold and hot wallets are further divided into different types. Let us take a look at the specific types of bitcoin wallets:

➢ Web wallet

Also known as an online or Internet wallet, a web wallet is a kind of hot wallet that you can use. This is also the most common wallet used by a majority of bitcoin users. A good example of a web wallet is Coinbase.

➢ Mobile wallet

A mobile wallet is just like a web wallet, but it is something that you can download on your mobile device. It is also a form of a hot wallet. Many web wallets are considered mobile wallets. A mobile wallet comes in the form of a downloadable application. There are many hot wallet sites that you can access using your mobile device.

➢ Desktop wallet

This is also referred to as a computer wallet. This is a kind of cold wallet where you store your bitcoins in a computer. Although usually called as a desktop wallet, it does not necessarily have to be a desktop computer. A laptop computer will do just fine.

Keep in mind that when you use a desktop wallet, you should not connect your computer to the Internet. The reason is that connecting your computer to the web will expose it to risks of getting hacked or compromised. There are many hackers and scammers online who are constantly looking for their next victim. You also do not need to use a new computer. An old computer with a well-functioning operating system will do just fine. Keep in mind that before you use it as a cold wallet, it is strongly advised that you reformat it to ensure that it is free of bugs and viruses.

➢ Hardware wallet

A hardware wallet is another kind of cold wallet. It is similar to a desktop wallet but instead of storing your bitcoins in a computer, you keep them in some form of hardware, such as a USB device. Again, be sure that the hardware where you intend to keep your bitcoins should be free of bugs and viruses. Hence, if you intend to use an old

USB device, then it is best to reformat it before you use it as a cold wallet.

➢ Paper wallet

A paper wallet is another popular kind of cold wallet. It is called a paper wallet because you keep and print your private keys on paper. It is suggested to have several copies and store them in a safe place.

Which type of bitcoin wallet should you use?

There is no hard and fast rule as to which bitcoin wallet you should use. The thing is to strike a good balance between convenience as offered by a hot wallet, and the security offered by a cold wallet. If you think that you will be sending and/orreceiving bitcoins regularly, then you might want to use a hot wallet. If you just want to store bitcoins for a long time in the form of an investment, then you may want to use a cold wallet. There are also bitcoin users who use both types of wallets at the same time. You can use a hot wallet for your day-to-day transactions and also keep a cold wallet for a long-term investment.

When you use a cold wallet, be sure to use something that has a good quality. If it gets broken, then it may be impossible to recover your bitcoins. Also, be sure to keep your cold wallet in a safe place. If it gets stolen, then you may no longer be able to recover your bitcoins. As you can see, even a cold wallet has its risks. It is also worth noting that many bitcoin users are already satisfied with a hot wallet. The good news is that the security offered by trusted and reliable hot wallets have already developed over time.

Bitcoin wallet protection tips

Here are notable tips to improve and ensure the security of your bitcoin wallet:

➢ Enhanced password

Your password is the first and main line of defense against hackers. Therefore, it is of primary importance that you use a strong password. But, what makes a strong password? There are certain guidelines for you to remember: Use a password that is hard to predict. Do not use your name or birth date as your password. Also, the longer your password is, the better. A common mistake is to only use the minimum number of characters. Also, you should combine upper and lower cases. You should also add some symbols and numbers to further increase the security of your account. It is also suggested that you update (change) your password from time to time.

➤ Request for a new wallet address

A single bitcoin wallet can generate multiple wallet addresses. Over the blockchain, your name or your bitcoin wallet itself will not be shown. It is only your bitcoin wallet address that will be revealed. You can request for a new bitcoin wallet address with just a click of a mouse, and this is free of charge. To minimize your exposure which, in turn, will minimize your risks, you should make it a habit of requesting for a new wallet address each time you make a transaction.

➤ Check if the page is secure

Before you key in your password or any sensitive information, check if the page is secure. This is easy to do: Simply look at the URL bar, and you should see a green padlock and/or the word "Secure." This signifies that it is safe to enter sensitive information like your bitcoin wallet address. This is a preventive measure against phishing sites or sites that duplicate a legitimate website to steal information.

➢ Avoid accessing your bitcoin wallet over a public Wi-Fi

Although a public Wi-Fi can be very convenient to use, it is not advisable when you want to access your bitcoin wallet. Connecting to a public Wi-Fi can be risky. Some hackers take advantage of public Wi-Fis. If you just want to surf the web, then there is nothing wrong with using a public Wi-Fi, but if you want to use access and manage your bitcoin wallet, especially if you need to key in sensitive information, then doing so over a public Wi-Fi is not a safe choice.

➢ Use multiple wallets

You have probably heard the saying, "Do not put all your eggs in one basket." The same advice is true when you use bitcoin wallets. Unfortunately, there have been reports of bitcoin wallets getting hacked. To minimize your risk, you should learn to spread your risk by using multiple wallets. This is true, especially if you are using a hot wallet. For example, instead of storing 3 bitcoins in a single hot wallet, store 1 bitcoin in a Coinbase wallet, another 1 bitcoin in another hot wallet like GreenAddress, and the remaining 1 bitcoin in a cold wallet.

➢ Keep your cold wallet in a safe place

Although cold wallets have a higher security since they are not connected to the Internet, they are still vulnerable to being stolen or destroyed. Make sure to keep your cold wallet in a safe place.

Chapter 4:

Make Money

Let us look at the different ways to make money with bitcoin. In fact, the main reason why many people are attracted to bitcoin is that of the amount of money that they can earn. The more bitcoins that you have, the more cash you can make.

Free faucet

This is the easiest way to earn your first bitcoins. If you are new to bitcoins and just want to experience having your own bitcoins, then you can take advantage of free faucets. A faucet will give you a small amount of bitcoin for free. You can find countless of bitcoin faucets online. You cannot expect to get rich simply by relying on faucets. A bitcoin faucet usually gives out a small amount of bitcoins on a regular basis. On average, you can expect to earn around 0.00000100 bitcoins per hour. This is not really an effective way to earn money, but it is a good way to make you earn your first bitcoins quickly and easily without any investment.

Bitcoin mining

Before any block is added to the chain, the transaction must first be confirmed and verified by miners. A miner receives a reward for mining. Mining is important to introduce a new block into the system. Without mining, transactions will remain unconfirmed and will not be completed. Since miners earn bitcoins as a reward, mining is also a good way to earn more bitcoins, which you can then convert into cash. There are generally two ways three ways to mine for bitcoins: (1) You can mine using your own computer; (2) You can mine using a hardware; and (3) You can mine using cloud mining.

Mining using your own computer is no longer suggested since you will most likely spend more money on electricity than the amount of bitcoins that you can earn for mining. To earn a significant amount of bitcoins, you need to have a higher hash mining power. To do this, you have two choices: mine using a hardware or over the cloud.

Chapter 4: Make Money

➢ Hardware mining

Mining using your computer alone is not enough. To make a good profit, you need to use a hardwareto increase your hash rate, which will allow you to earn more bitcoins. If you choose to do hardware mining, you need to purchase a good hardware for mining. Now, there are many different choices of hardware that you can choose from. Of course, a hardware that will give you more mining power will be more expensive. When you mine with a hardware, you still have to use your computer. Therefore, hardware mining means mining using your computer and a hardware at the same time.

The drawback to hardware mining is the issue of overheating. Since you will have to mine for hours on a regular basis using your computer and mining hardware, overheating can be a problem. Worse, it can break your computer and your hardware in the long run, which would mean additional expenses for you. If you intend to use hardware mining, you will have to follow a certain schedule for mining and always give time for your computer and mining hardware to cool down.

➢ Cloud mining

Cloud mining is the type of bitcoin mining that is getting popular these days. With cloud mining, you will no longer have to buy a hardware. In fact, you do not even have to turn on your computer just to mine for bitcoins. When you use cloud mining, a mining company will do all the work for you. All that you need to do is wait for the mining company to send your bitcoins to your wallet. A good example of a cloud mining company is Genesis Mining. Normally, you will have to pay a mining company a certain amount. For example, deposit/pay 1 bitcoin and get 0.08 bitcoins every week. This will depend upon the agreement that you have with the mining company. There are also mining companies that will allow you to buy as many hash power rate as you want, and they will give you the expected equivalent bitcoins that you can get from them, depending on the number of the hash rate that you purchase.

Okay, so this looks like the best deal. But, what is the drawback, if any? The drawback is that what the mining company shows you is usually just the expected return and not the actual return that you will get. Hence, even if a mining company says that you can expect to get 0.08 bitcoins every week, you may end up only receiving 0.05 per week. Be sure that the terms and conditions of the contract are clear to you before you spend any real money. Also, be careful of scammers online. There have been reports where investors do not receive any bitcoins at all from a mining company. Be sure to work only with trusted and reliable mining company. You are expected to always do your research and pay attention to the latest ratings and reviews of a mining company before you deposit real money/cryptocurrency in your account.

Is bitcoin mining still profitable? It depends. The problem with mining bitcoins is that it will take time for you to recover your investment. Most experts suggest that if you are serious about earning money with bitcoin, then the best way is for you to study and learn how to invest in and trade bitcoin.

Bitcoin gambling

If you are fond of casino gambling, then bitcoin offers excellent online casino experience. In fact, bitcoin has its own gambling game known as Dice. Why would you want to gamble with bitcoin? Aside from the fact that there are many bitcoin casinos online, there are other good reasons on why you would want to gamble using bitcoin. Unlike other online casinos, you can deposit and withdraw bitcoin almost instantly. As for withdrawal, you will usually receive your bitcoins in your wallet in just a few minutes. In case you are withdrawing a big amount, you can still expect to receive your withdrawal in less than 24 hours. Normally, when you play casino online and withdraw funds to your bank, it will take days for a single transaction to be completed. With bitcoin, transactions get confirmed and completed quickly.

Most bitcoin casinos also have a provably fair system. What it does is to let you ensure that the outcome of a game is fair and without any form of bias or undue influence.

Bitcoin casinos also offer live casinos where you will be served by a live, beautiful, and professional dealer. Whether you want to play baccarat, blackjack, or roulette, you will definitely find a dealer for you. Most live casinos also gave a chat feature, which will allow you to talk with the dealer in real time. This way you can be sure that the games are not pre-recorded and that everything is actually happening in real time.

Still, casino gambling is not an advisable way to make money with bitcoin considering that most gamblers lose their money quickly or in the long run. If you think that you have a system that can beat the casino's house edge or if you simply want to try your luck, then bitcoin casinos will definitely give you a convenient and exciting experience.

Bitcoin trading

Bitcoin trading, or more specifically, cryptocurrency trading, is the most popular way to make money with bitcoin quickly. This works just like the typical forex, but you will have to deal with different cryptocurrencies. Therefore, this approach requires a good amount of research and analysis.

Another form of trading is binary options trading. There are many sites online that will allow you to do binary trading with bitcoin. Binary options are the closest that you can get to casino gambling as you can trade binary in as fast as one minute or even 30 seconds. Although you can still make money with binary options, it is not as easy as it may seem. In fact, themajority of people who invest in binary options end up losing their money. If you ever intend to focus on binary trading, then be sure to learn and use proper strategies.

Bitcoin investing

This is the most common way to make money with bitcoin. The main factor that creates the profit is the increasing price of bitcoin. For example, if had you invested in bitcoin in the early part of 2017, then you would have gained a profit of more than 100‰ of your original investment by now. The most common strategy when investing in bitcoin is the buy and hold strategy. As the name implies, you simply have to buy bitcoins, and then hold on to them as you wait for their price to increase. You can then sell them for profit in the future. If you do not want to get too technical, then this strategy is the one for you. Had you applied this strategy way back in 2010 even with just a $400 investment, then you would have been a multimillionaire by now.

Chapter 4: Make Money

Investing in bitcoin is actually very easy to do. All that you need is to get a bitcoin wallet, buy bitcoins, keep them in your wallet, and wait for the price of bitcoin to increase. This is all about the common principle that states: "Buy low, sell high."

The price of bitcoin can fluctuate significantly even within a 24-hour timeline. Therefore, proper timing should be observed before you make any buy order. A suggested way to do this is to study the recent trend of bitcoin and see if making a buy order at this very moment would be a good choice or should you wait for a few more hours. With enough research, you will be able to predict to theright time to buy bitcoins. Usually, the best time to make a buy order is before or immediately right after a certain promotion or event about bitcoin is made. The more positive attention is given to bitcoin, the more likely its price will increase. Hence, if you think the price of bitcoin will increase, then make a buy order; if you think that its price will decrease, then make a sell order.

Chapter 5:

Bitcoin Investing/Trading Strategies

Fundamental analysis

Fundamental analysis is also referred to as the lifeblood of investment. This is how essential this strategy is. The reason is that this strategy deals with the basics. As the name implies, it focuses on the fundamentals. When you deal with bitcoins and use fundamental analysis, you will have to examine and analyze the different factors that affect the price of bitcoin, such as market behavior, competition among the different cryptocurrencies, news updates, legalities, economy, latest trends and technological developments, among others.

No matter which strategy you use, fundamental analysis remains vital as it can be used to justify your investment decision. Fortunately, this strategy is something that you can apply and combine with another strategy. It always helps to know and understand what is going on in the bitcoin and cryptocurrency economy. The more that you understand the different factors that affect the price of bitcoin, the more easily you can predict its price movement.

So, before you make any trade or investment, take some time to analyze the situation. Look at the different factors that affect the price of bitcoin. When you do fundamental analysis, then you need to be ready to make some serious research. Again, the key to this strategy is to get as much basic information as you can. Once you have the fundamentals sorted out, then you will have a better view of the market. This will allow you to make a better investment or trading decision. You should also understand that the price of bitcoin does not fluctuate at random. It just so happens that many factors affect its price movement, but it is never left to chance. Therefore, by taking the time to understand these factors, you will be able to better predict its price behavior. Once you can foresee how its price will move, then you can take appropriate actions (buy or sell bitcoins) for profit.

If you see yourself as a serious investor or trader, then fundamental analysis should be a part of your everyday life. Always be updated on the news and learn as much as you can about everything that can be connected to bitcoin.

Fundamental analysis does not end with just getting the facts. Another vital step is for you to properly analyze the details that you have. Be careful not to be biased in your judgment. You should look at the facts from an unbiased and impartial perspective. This way you can have a better view of what is actually going on in the bitcoin market and identify the best move to take.

Technical analysis

This is a favorite approach of many investors and traders. Unlike fundamental analysis that deals with hard facts and numbers, technical analysis deals with graphs and charts. So, if you are more of a visual person, then this strategy is for you. The graphs and charts reflect the price movements of bitcoin. The concept behind this strategy is that the different factors that influence the price movements of bitcoin have their final effect on the price. Therefore, simply by analyzing the price movements and fluctuations, you also get to deal with all the other factors that affect bitcoin.

When you use technical analysis, you should learn to recognize and read patterns. It should be noted that patterns come and go. Nonetheless, they still happen from time to time. A common mistake committed by many traders is to see a pattern even when no pattern actually exists. Keep in mind that you should never force a pattern. Just because you look at a certain graph for more than 20 minutes does not mean that there is always a pattern or trend to be seen. If you are truly able to identify a certain trend, then you should take advantage of it. Even a random generator still forms patterns from time to time. The key to profit is to be able to identify a pattern and take advantage of it before it disappears.

Just like fundamental analysis, you can combine technical analysis with other strategies. Since technical analysis deals with graphs and charts, you can use this approach as a tool to get additional information. But, where do you get these graphs and charts? Ideally, it is your broker that should provide you with these helpful tools. If your broker does not provide the said graphs, then you can visit bitcoin and other cryptocurrency websites to see charts that show the price behavior of bitcoin, as well as other cryptocurrencies. Although there are people who believe that technical analysis alone is enough to provide you with all the information that you need to come up with a sound investment decision, this book encourages that you use technical analysis together with fundamental analysis.

Go with the flow

A few months ago, there was positive news about bitcoin that was featured on CNN. As can be expected, the price of bitcoin increased. After some time, there was news about China closing down its local cryptocurrency exchanges, and the price of bitcoin dropped. As you can see, the price movement of bitcoin is not that difficult to predict. A good news about bitcoin results in an increase in price, while a bad news on bitcoin tends to pull its price down. The key to the go with the flow strategy is to be updated on the latest news and respond accordingly. For example, if good news is being promoted about bitcoin, then you can expect for bitcoin's price to increase. Conversely, if there is any bad news about bitcoin, then it will most probably experience a decrease in value. By understanding the news, you will be able to tell the best time to make a buy or sell order. When it comes to investing and trading, proper timing is very important.

Averaging down

This strategy is an effective way to earn a significant amount of bitcoins. You need to be careful as this is considered an aggressive approach. Here is an example of how this strategy works: Let us say that the price of 1 bitcoin is equivalent to $5,000. You then make a buy order at the said price of $5,000. Now, let us assume that its price falls to $4,900, you then make another buy order at the said lower price of $4,900. Again, let us say that its price drops down to $4,750, you should make another buy order at the said price, and so on and so forth. By doing so, you get to buy it at a bargain each time you make a buy order. But, what a second, are you not buying a losing asset? In a way, yes, you are buying bitcoin while its price is falling down. This may be counter-intuitive. Try to imagine what will happen if its price shoots back up to its original price (the price when you first applied the strategy), then all the buy orders that you have made will turn into a profitable investment and experience a nice profit. This is actually the key to profit of the averaging down strategy. It takes advantage of the high volatility of bitcoin. Keep in mind to be careful when you use this approach as it is also possible for the price of bitcoin to experience a serious and constant downfall. Therefore, before you even use this strategy, be sure to do all the necessary research and analysis.

Quick sell

This strategy aims to earn a little bit of profit several times. You should be content with small gains. To make a decent income, you need to invest a huge amount of bitcoins. Here is an example of how this strategy works: Let us say that you have 1 bitcoin in your trading account. Once you see that the price of bitcoin increases during the day, then you make a sell order and enjoy your small profit from the transaction. Fortunately, the price of bitcoin fluctuates significantly within a 24-hour timeline. You simply have to repeat this process as much as you can. When you use this strategy, you have to avoid getting greedy. Instead, you should be content with a small amount of profit. This strategy also does not have any risk as you are sure to make a profit when you sell your bitcoins. All that you need to do is to have some bitcoins in your account, be patient, and sell your bitcoins for profit.

Is there a difference between investing and trading?

Many people use these terms synonymously. Whether investing and trading are the same or different depends on how you view it. For starters, you can say that trading entails a more active approach. After all, you can make multiple trades in a single day. Investing, on the other hand, entails a more passive approach where you simply buy something and wait for the right time to sell it for profit. When you invest in something, you will also trade it sooner or later to make a profit, and when you trade something, you also have to invest some money into the venture. From this perspective, then trading and investing can be considered closely similar. This book uses both terms synonymously. According to an expert, "It does not matter whether you see yourself as an investor or trader, the important thing is how much profit you make, if any."

Chapter 6:

Bitcoin Trading Broker

What to look for in a bitcoin trading broker

I f you want to trade bitcoins, then you should work with a reliable and trusted broker. Doing a simple search online will give you a list of different brokers that seem to offer the same services. So, how do you know which broker will best suit your needs? Here are the standards to look for:

Latest ratings and reviews

Make sure to check the latest ratings and reviews of a trading broker before you deposit any money. You can easily do this by using your favorite search engine. Just type the name of the broker and add the word "reviews." Press the enter key, and the search engine results pages (SERP) will give you a list of related pages.

Cryptocurrency

Carefully read the reviews and take note of the dates when they were made. Also, it is not uncommon for brokers to hire a freelance writer to write a positive review about them, so do not just rely on a single website for reviews. Most legitimate reviews are those that also mention something negative about a broker. If a review seems too good to be true, then it is probably is. The more references and reviews that you read about a particular broker, the better.

Customer support

You should work with a broker that has a professional and responsive customer support. What are the ways that you can contact the support team? Is there a beer that you can call at any time or is there a live chat schedule? Most brokers can be contacted via email. Make sure that a broker's customer support team responds quickly. A good way to find out is to test it before you even make an account or before making a deposit. Just send a message to the support team and ask any legitimate question. Try to see how professionally they handle your inquiry, as well as how many days it will take them to resolve it.

Chapter 6: Bitcoin Trading Broker

Margin trading

Margin trading is where you can borrow bitcoins from your broker. In exchange, you will have to pay interest. Normally, a broker will allow you to margin trade more than 50‰ of your investment. This is a good way to earn a nice profit, especially if you do not have a big capital. Although margin trading is a good way to earn more profit, be cautious of using it as it can be a problem and a liability in the long run. If you ever make use of margin trading, then be sure to adapt a strategy that is suitable for it.

Mobile feature

Your broker's trading platform should be accessible on your mobile device. These days, the most convenient way to access the Internet is not with the use of a computer, but with your mobile phone. Do not worry; all trusted brokers have a mobile feature. The mobile version should also be easy to navigate, and it should allow you to access the important parts and features of the trading platform.

Design and layout

Although not required, it still helps if the trading platform is professionally designed. It must have a layout that is easy and convenient to navigate. Simple yet professionally designed layouts are best for this. Navigating the platform should be easy and intuitive. The important parts of the trading platform should be properly sorted and easily accessible.

Fees

You should be aware of the transaction fee that is imposed by your broker. A broker usually charges a fee per trade and every time you make a withdrawal. Although this may only involve a small amount, it can quickly add up into a significant amount in the long run.

Promos and bonuses

Brokers usually reward their traders with promos and bonuses. Pay close attention to the terms and conditions before you accept a bonus. For example, a broker may offer you a 50% bonus. But, the drawback is that before you can make a withdrawal, you will have to trade the bonus 35 times, or even more. For most people, they tend to lose their entire bankroll before they even meet the requirement to cash out the bonus/promo. If you think that you cannot satisfy the requirement, then it would be better if you do not accept the bonus.

Deposit and withdrawal limit

It is also suggested that you check the minimum and maximum deposit and withdrawal that is allowed by your broker. This information is usually found on the Banking page. If you cannot find it, do not hesitate to contact your broker.

Required documents

It is not uncommon for brokers to ask for certain documents like valid IDs and proof of billing before they process a withdrawal. Be sure that you have these documents in your possession. Brokers do not usually ask for such documents when you make a deposit, but they usually require them when you make a withdrawal. If you do not have the required documents, contact the customer support team and ask for substitute documents that you can submit to them. Make sure that this part is clear to you before you even make a deposit; otherwise, you will run the risk of having your bitcoins locked in your trading account without any way of withdrawing them.

Demo account

Most reputable brokers will provide you with a demo account. A demo account will allow you to trade bitcoins and other cryptocurrencies in a real and live market without any risk. Of course, you will not earn any real income from it, but you can use the demo account to test your strategy, as well as to familiarize yourself with the actual trading environment. If a demo account is not provided by your broker, what you can do is to open an account with another broker just to take advantage of a demo account. If you want, you can just switch completely to another broker. Another option that you have is simply to trade with very small amounts to minimize your risks.

Do I need a trading broker?

You do not always need a broker to make money with bitcoin. In fact, the only reason why you may want to use a broker is if you intend to trade cryptocurrencies. If you just want to invest in bitcoin, then you do not need to have a broker. Many investors just use their hot wallets to store their bitcoins, and then they sell them after some time for profit. Simply put, if you do not want to trade cryptocurrencies, then you do not need a broker. For the mere purpose of investing in bitcoin, all that you need is a bitcoin wallet.

Chapter 7:

Best Practices

Sufficient research

Make sure that you do enough research before you invest any real money in anything. This is not just about doing a research. You need to be sure to do *sufficient* research. This means that the amount and quality of information that you have should be sufficient to help you come up with a sound investment decision. It is true that no matter how hard you research on something, there is still no guarantee that you will end up with a positive profit; however, do not forget that the more that you know and understand bitcoin, the more likely that you will be able to predict its price movement. Still, remember, there is no 100% guarantee of making a successful trade or investment despite the amount of research that you make. Taking risks is part of the game. If you do sufficient amount of research, then you significantly increase your chances of making a profit.

Bitcoin trading journal

Although not a requirement, having a bitcoin trading journal can be a useful tool. You do not need to be a professional writer to write a journal. You have to update your journal regularly and be completely honest with everything that you write in your journal.

A journal will allow you to see yourself from a new perspective that is free from any form of bias or prejudice. You should make it a habit to update your journal truthfully and regularly for it shall serve as a mirror of yourself as a trader/investor. Ideally, your journal should contain your strategies, objectives, mistakes, and lessons, as well as a record of your trades. Since it is your own personal journal, feel free to record in your journal everything that is related to your activity as a bitcoin investor/trader.

When you read your journal, you will be able to envision yourself from a clearer perspective. Do not hesitate to make adjustments and work on flaws that you may see in your current strategy.

Also, focus on further developing your strengths. Although writing a journal can be quite time-consuming, the benefits and lessons that you can get from it are well worth every effort that you put into your journal.

Money management

How you manage your money is important to your success. Poor money management can cause you to lose all your investment. Therefore, you need to have a plan. A good way to do this is to write down your plan and objectives on a paper or in a notebook. Know how much you are willing to invest in bitcoin, as well as how much profit you expect to make. Make your plans reasonable. Although investing in bitcoin usually gives positive returns, it is still an investment. Therefore, you should also be ready to face some risks. As a rule, you should only invest the money that you can afford to lose. Therefore, do not invest the money that you need to pay for your household bills and other obligations. You should have a plan on how much money you are willing to invest, as well as how you intend to use the bitcoin in your account.

Analyzing expert advice

People who are new to bitcoin usually rely on the pieces of advice given by so-called experts. They usually read their articles, books, and blog posts. The sad truth is that many of these so-called experts are real experts when it comes to making money with bitcoin. Especially in today's age, it is very easy to promote one's self as an expert on social media with just a click of a mouse. Of course, there are also real experts out there, but even these true experts also commit mistakes from time to time. Instead of completely relying on expert advice, what you need to do is to form your own understanding of the bitcoin market. Instead of believing everything that the experts are saying, you should try to examine and analyze their point of view. Remember: Never make any investment simply because an expert has told you to do so. As a beginner, it is good to read as much as you can about bitcoin and visit related blogs and sites. Do not forget that you should develop your own understanding of bitcoin. Not to mention, even the real experts themselves also have conflicting views from time to time.

Take a break

You should give yourself time to take a break and relax from time to time. Remember that you will be more able to think more clearly and objectively if you give yourself time to relax. The best way to relax is to do something that is not related to bitcoin trading and investing. It is also important that you do not think of anything that is related to bitcoin during the time that you are relaxing. This is the best time for you to go on a vacation with your family. After all, being a professional investor can be a busy job; you deserve to enjoy and have fun from time to time. The good thing about this is that your mind will be more refreshed the moment you get back to work, which will allow you to think more clearly and come up with a sound investment decision. As an investor, you have full control of your time. Needless to say, do not abuse this prerogative. Remember that you should take a break to allow you to recover from too much work and not because you are feeling lazy to work.

Withdraw

Many investors and traders do not withdraw their profits on the reasoning that if they do not withdraw their profits, then they will have a bigger fund that they can use for trading/investing. Therefore, the profit potential will also be higher. Although this point is reasonable, it is still important to withdraw and cash out your profits from time to time. After all, you do not have to withdraw all your profits at once. If you want, you can just withdraw 30% of your total profits every week. This is a matter of personal preference, but the important thing is for you to make a withdrawal from time to time. The reason is that no matter how much profit you make, it will not be completely realized until you turn it into cash. To do so, you need to make a withdrawal. Another reason is that making a withdrawal minimizes your losses. Once you withdraw and turn your bitcoins into cash, then they are no longer exposed to the risks that naturally present in a trading environment. If you just come to think of it, if you do not withdraw your profits, then it is almost the same as if you were using a mere demo account. Therefore, do not forget to cash out even just a portion of your overall profits from time to time.

Join groups and forums

Being updated on the news is a good way to receive information about bitcoin. However, news about bitcoin is not limited to what is shown on the news. By joining bitcoin and cryptocurrency groups and forums online, you will be able to get more information. In fact, many updates about bitcoin and other cryptocurrencies first appear in online groups and forums before they turn into news headlines or clips. The reason is that even the developers of many cryptocurrencies are active in online groups and forums. Therefore, if you are serious about making money with bitcoin, then it is strongly suggested that you join and participate in online groups and forums on bitcoin, as well as other cryptocurrency. Another advantage of joining such groups is to learn other interesting ideas and perspectives from other investors and traders.

Test your strategy

Test your strategy several times before you apply it using real money/cryptocurrency. No matter how much you read about a certain strategy, the only way to learn how to apply it properly is by actual application. If you want to be a professional trader, then you should know that working on your strategy is a life-long journey. If you hate continuously developing a strategy, then perhaps being a trader is not for you. Your strategy is an important part of your activities as a trader. You are expected to work on your strategy continuously. Do not forget that bitcoin is highly volatile, and so your strategy should be able to adapt to changes in the environment.

There appears to be no strategy that can work for all types of situations. You need to be flexible enough and adapt to changes. You should also remember that even if you just change a minor part of your strategy, then you should give it a series of tests before applying it using real money. When you are a trader or investor, you should understand that a slight change in a strategy can create a big difference. Therefore, always remember to test your strategy.

Wait it out

Never make decisions when you are under pressure. Also, in case the market is in panic, you should learn to be calm. It is normal for an investment to face some complications or problems from time to time. If the thing where you invested your money in is truly valuable, then it will be able to recover after some time. As an investor, sometimes the best way to face a difficult time is simply to wait it out. If you examine the past trends of bitcoin, you will see that it also faced certain problems, such as when Russia considered it to be illegal. Today, Russia is one of the supporters of bitcoin. If the price of bitcoin drops significantly, many investors begin to panic. You should not be like them. Instead, learn to be patient and understand the real situation. Moreover, during times when you do not know the best move to take, remember that sometimes the best action is simply to wait it out.

Right understanding of high volatility

When people describe bitcoin, one of the things that they will certainly mention is its high volatility. However, what does it really mean when you say that something has a high volatility? Simply put, high volatility only means that the price changes significantly within a short period of time. But, how does it change? Many people think that a drop in price will soon be followed by a high increase in price. Conversely, a high increase in price will soon be followed by a significant decrease in price. It is as if it will balance itself out in the long run. This is not what high volatility is, especially the high volatility of bitcoin. When you deal with bitcoin, you should understand that a series of increase can still follow a high increase in price, and a decrease in price can still be followed by another significant drop in value. You cannot expect the price to balance itself out even in the long run. The price of bitcoin is not something that just comes at random, but it depends on many factors.

Professional approach

There are people who approach bitcoin trading/investing as a hobby. Although there is nothing wrong with this, you should also not expect to get a high amount of profit. If you just want to deal with bitcoin as a mere hobby, a good suggestion is simply for you to follow the buy and hold strategy instead of actively trading bitcoins with other cryptocurrencies. If you trade bitcoins, then you should also have a good understanding of other cryptocurrencies.

If you are serious about making money with bitcoin, then you should approach it professionally. This means that you should be dedicated and committed to it. Usually, people who only take it as a hobby do not exercise enough discipline, and so they fail to make any decent profit. Although there is still no guarantee that you will make a good amount of profit if you approach it professionally, it is certain that following a professional approach can significantly increase your chances of making positive returns. Now, in case that you want to trade bitcoins but simply do not have enough time to study the market, the best suggestion is for you to make just a few trades. When it comes to bitcoin trading and investing, you should never rely completely on luck. Of course, luck can give you profits from time to time, but you cannot expect for it alone to keep you in a positive profit in the long run.

Start small

Even if you have lots of bitcoins in your account, it is good to start small. This is true, especially if you engage in cryptocurrency trading. As a beginner, your first objective is not to make money right away but simply to familiarize yourself with the trading environment. Starting out with a small amount is also a good way to avoid being an emotional trader.

Do not be an emotional trader/investor

Never allow your emotions to dictate your decisions. Being an investor or trader can be a sad life. It is the kind of life where nobody cares even if you lose all your money at once. The market does not care about you; the bitcoin cryptocurrency does not even know you at all. This is the kind of life where everything is purely business without any need for human interaction. The whole process of trading or investing happens online and usually with just a few clicks of a mouse. From then on, all that you need to do is wait and hope for the best.

To avoid being an emotional trader, you should not be attached to your bitcoins. Hence, make sure not to invest the money that you cannot afford to lose. Also, never panic. The moment you notice that you are not thinking clearly, then learn to stop and just relax for a while. Do not make rush decisions. If you want to have any success with cryptocurrency trading, then learn to control yourself, and always make decisions objectively.

Continuous practice

Success in trading or investing in bitcoin is not something that you master simply by reading books. Every true investor/trader knows the importance of continuous practice. You may want to use your broker's demo account to practice. Of course, every actual trade that you make is also part of the practice. Take the time to stop and reflect upon the effects of every transaction that you make.

Chapter 8:

The Future of Bitcoin

Nobody can tell for sure what the future of bitcoin will be. If you look at its past and present trends, it is easy to see that a bright future awaits it. More and more people are being open to the use of bitcoin, as proven by the fact that its price is continuously rising. Today, even governments are taking interest in bitcoin. In some states, you can now pay for your electric and other household bills in bitcoins. In the Philippines, you can convert your bitcoins into cash and enjoy cardless withdrawal at selected ATMs. In other states, you can now book a hotel room and even purchase an airfare ticket online using bitcoin.

Many experts say that the price of bitcoin is expected to reach more than $10,000 for 1 bitcoin in less than two years. Bitcoin is continuously gaining population and attention, and more and more people are drawn to it. In the future, it is expected that banks will have a separate account for bitcoins. Some even claim that bitcoin, as powered by its blockchain, will soon take the place of banks and will take the form of a one-world cryptocurrency. After all, we now live in a computer and Internet generation, and bitcoin is the money of the Internet.

It is not just bitcoin that you should watch out for. Blockchain technology, the backbone technology of bitcoin, is also gaining popularity and worldwide interest. Experts found that this technology is not only applicable to financial services but can also be used for other purposes.

Indeed, the bitcoin revolution is changing the world. Among all the cryptocurrencies in the world, it is only bitcoin that demonstrates a constant positive development. Today, more and more people want to learn about bitcoin. It is this kind of attention and curiosity that works well in favor of bitcoin. Now, it is common for bitcoin users to promote bitcoin on social media. Usually, bitcoin is promoted as a form of a lucrative investment and not just as a substitute for money. After all, bitcoin is, indeed, a lucrative investment. Instead of investing in stocks where a profit of 15% per year is already considered to be high, this 15% can be earned in a few days or even in a single day if you invest in bitcoin.

What the future holds remains a mystery for bitcoin. Although things seem to appear promising for bitcoin, you should not underestimate the fact that there are still risks involved when you deal with bitcoin. There is a possibility that bitcoin may just disappear completely without any warning. Just like any other investment, there is a chance for you to turn bitcoin into a goldmine of profit but there is also a risk that you can lose your investment. The good news is that if you just look at the trend, it is easy to see that bitcoin remains to be a lucrative investment. In fact, you do not even need to do anything complicated. A simple but and hold approach will be enough for you to enjoy profits from your investment in bitcoin. The price of bitcoin is continuously increasing while more and more people are becoming more aware of it and learning about it. Indeed, there are good reasons to believe that the price of bitcoin will constantly increase in the coming months or even years.

Cryptocurrency

The classic example that if you invested even just $500 in bitcoins in 2010, then you would have been a multimillionaire by now remains true even today. Although you may not be a multimillionaire if you just invest $500, the chances are that you can still expect to realize some nice profits.

Bitcoin is the key to financial freedom. The future will depend on what you do today. Merely reading about bitcoin is not enough. For you to enjoy all the benefits and profits that it brings, you need to take positive actions. So, invest in bitcoin today and live a happier and successful life.

Conclusion

T hanks for making it through to the end of this book. We hope it was informative and able to provide you with all of the tools you need to achieve your goals whatever they may be.

The next step is to apply everything that you have learned and start earning real profits by investing in and trading bitcoin. Reading books and articles on the subject is an important step to learning how you can turn bitcoin into a goldmine. However, reading alone is not enough. Another important step that you should take is to apply your knowledge. Since you have reached this part of the book, it is safe to assume that you already have enough knowledge on how you can make money with bitcoins. Remember to observe the teachings in this book, especially the best practices. Unfortunately, some people get too greedy and end up losing their investment. Do not be like them. Again, it bears stressing that if you intend to make serious profits with bitcoin, then you should take it seriously and professionally.

Bitcoin can offer the doors to financial freedom. It is continuously gaining popularity, and people from around the globe are being more open to it. The good news is that this kind of promotion can lead to significant increases in its value. The more people are drawn and get interested in bitcoin, the higher is the probability for its price to take an upward swing.

Although bitcoin is gaining worldwide attention, it is still fairly new in the market. We can still expect some more improvements and developments in the future. That means you have to make sure self prepared for the possible problems that you may encounter with Bitcoin. Remember, the developers of this currency are not perfect, there could be system issues that may occur from time to time. If so, seek help from the professionals. You might want to reach out to the Bitcoin geeks that can help you solve your problems. Nobody knows what Bitcoin will become in the future. No one knows if this new currency will soar high like a bird. But we can be positive about the outcomes. As more and more people use and trust Bitcoin, we can be confident that Bitcoin's future shines as bright as the sun. It is still in the developing process, and as the time passes, more improvements are being implemented.

As an investment, there is no guarantee that investing in bitcoin today will rake in positive profits in the future. Just like any other investment, there is always the risk that you may end up losing your money. The good news is that if you look at the long-term trend of bitcoin, you will easily see that it is progressing positively and that you will most likely earn a nice profit if you stick to it. So far, the price of bitcoin has maintained its upward swing over the years. Of course, it is also subject to the usual fluctuations, but if you observe its long-term behavior, it cannot be denied that its price is taking a positive direction, which makes it a very lucrative investment. Now, is it already too late to invest in bitcoin? Clearly, the answer is *No*. In fact, if you analyze the current trend, you will easily find good reasons to believe that its price will continue to increase over the coming months as more and more people are supporting it.

By now, you should already have enough knowledge and understanding of what bitcoin is really all about. Now, it is time for you to journey and apply everything that you know about bitcoin. After all, knowledge without application is good for nothing.

Again, Bitcoin is not just another toy. It's a real currency that can either make you money or can turn you broke. Gather as much information as you need to fully understand the platform.

Finally, if you found this book useful in anyway, a review on Amazon is always appreciated!